I CAN READ ABOUT
WEATHER

Written by Robyn Supraner   Illustrated by Herbert Mott

Troll Associates

10 9 8 7 6 5 4 3

When you wake up in the morning, do you look out of the window to see what kind of day it's going to be?

Do you look up at the sky and wonder about the weather?

Some days are rainy.

Some days are cloudy and chilly.

And on some days, big, fat flakes of
snow come tumbling out of the sky.

All of these are different kinds of weather.
The air, all around you, is part of the weather, too.
So when you breathe in and when you breathe out,
you are breathing a piece of the weather.

There is some kind of weather in every part of the world. Somewhere, people are sunbathing. Somewhere else, a storm is raging. Thunder rumbles and lightning seems to crack the sky.

What makes the rain?
What makes the snow?
What makes different
kinds of weather?

All of our weather begins with the sun. When the sun shines, it warms everything it touches. This happens because the sun gives us heat.

You can feel the heat on
a sunny day at the beach.

You can feel the heat when you're going down on the slide.

When the sun shines,
something else happens.

Lakes and rivers and oceans grow
warmer. Ponds and pools grow warmer,
too. Clothes that were hung on the line
in the morning are *dry* by the afternoon.
Puddles dry up. The water seems to disappear.

What is happening?
The warm water is changing into a gas
called water vapor. The more the sun
shines, the faster the water evaporates.
It does not really disappear. It becomes
an invisible part of the air.

The warm air, with water vapor in it,
rises high above the earth, where the air
is cool. There, it changes into
millions of tiny drops of water.
The droplets bunch together.
They make a cloud.

Do you remember the last time you played outdoors on a very cold day? Do you remember the tiny clouds that formed every time you breathed out?

That was because your breath contains water vapor. When the warm water vapor was cooled by the chilly air, it changed into tiny droplets. It made a little cloud.

Big clouds are made
in much the same way.

Soft, fluffy clouds that look
like puffs of cotton are called
cumulus (kew-mew-lus) clouds.
When cumulus clouds sail the sky, the
weather will be fair. It is a good day
for a picnic.

PICNIC
GROUNDS →

Clouds that look feathery are called cirrus (seer-us) clouds. They are thin and wispy. They float so high in the sky that they have ice crystals in them.

When you see cirrus clouds, you had better pack an umbrella in your picnic basket. The weather just might change!

Light clouds. Thin clouds. Soft clouds. White clouds. These are the clouds that hold only a little water.

When we see them, we know that the weather will probably be nice.

But as millions and millions of water droplets gather together, the clouds get bigger and bigger. After a while, they get darker and darker. The drops of water get too heavy to stay up in the clouds. They fall back to earth, and we have rain!

Sometimes we have a light rain. But sometimes, the rain comes pouring down and the streets fill up like rivers.

Dark and heavy clouds are called
cumulo-nimbus (kew-mew-lō nim-bus) clouds.
When you see them, they tell you bad
weather is on the way. Sure enough,
here comes the rain!

Sometimes, high up in the air, the water vapor gets so cold that it freezes into beautiful, frosty crystals. These crystals are called snowflakes. When they fall, we have snow.

Each crystal has six sides,
and no two are ever alike.

Sometimes, the falling flakes pass through a layer of warm air. They melt and become drops of rain. The falling raindrops pass through more layers of air. These layers may be cold. Then the raindrops freeze into tiny pieces of ice. When they do, we have sleet or frozen rain!

Did you ever see a ball of ice fall out of the sky in the middle of July?

If you did, you have seen a hailstone. Hail comes out of a thunderstorm . . . the kind we usually get in summer.

High above the earth,
where the air is very cold,
drops of water freeze and
start to fall. But before
they can melt in the warm
air below, they are tossed
back into the upper air by
stormy winds, getting a
coat of water.

Up they go, and again they freeze. Again they start to fall. And again the gusty winds blow them high into the sky. Another coat of ice forms. The hailstones get bigger and bigger. This bouncing around can happen many times. Some hailstones get to be as big as baseballs!

At last, the balls of ice are so heavy
they fall to earth. When they do, we say
it is hailing.

Some clouds do not form in the sky. They form closer to earth. Then everything looks gray. Sometimes it is hard to see things that are right in front of you. When this happens, we have fog.

On some days, early in the morning, water vapor cools very close to the ground. Then the grass is covered with tiny, sparkling drops of water. When this happens, we have dew.

On very cold mornings, the water vapor freezes.
Then each blade of grass and every twig is lightly
iced with frozen crystals. When this happens,
we have frost.

Weather is an important part of our lives. A scientist who studies the weather is called a meteorologist (mēt-ē-a-ral-a-jest). A meteorologist studies the air and wind and rain, and makes forecasts about the weather.

Pilots must know what the weather will bring. Bad weather can be trouble.

Farmers depend on the sun and rain to grow healthy crops. An early frost can kill the farmer's crops before they can be harvested.

Thick fog can mean danger for cars
and boats.

But for children,
weather can be fun.
On warm, hot days, you
can go swimming.

On cold, chilly days,
you can go ice skating.

Just think of all the wonderful things you can do in all kinds of weather!